THE USBORNE
NURSERY RHYME
SONGBOOK

CAROLINE HOOPER

ILLUSTRATED BY RADHI PAREKH

DESIGNED BY
AMANDA BARLOW & KATHY WARD

Edited by Emma Danes
Music arrangements by Caroline Hooper

CONTENTS

LITTLE BOY BLUE

Lit - tle Boy Blue, come blow _ your horn, The sheep's in the mead -ow, the cow's in the corn; But where is the boy who looks af - ter the sheep? He's un -der a hay __ stack, fast a - sleep. Will you wake him? No, not I, For if I do, __ he's sure to cry.

Little Boy Blue, come blow your horn,
The sheep's in the meadow, the cow's in the corn;
But where is the boy who looks after the sheep?
He's under a haystack, fast asleep.
Will you wake him? No, not I,
For if I do, he's sure to cry.

IF ALL THE WORLD WERE PAPER

If all the world were paper,
And all the sea were ink,
If all the trees were bread and cheese,
What should we have to drink?

RUB-A-DUB-DUB

Rub-a-dub-dub, Three men in a tub, And who do you think they be? The but-cher, the ba-ker, The can-dle-stick-ma-ker, So turn out the knaves, all three.

Rub-a-dub-dub,
Three men in a tub,
And who do you think they be?
The butcher, the baker,
The candlestick-maker,
So turn out the knaves, all three.

JACK AND JILL

Jack and Jill went up the hill To fetch a pail of wa-ter;

Jack fell down and broke his crown, And Jill came tum-bling af-ter.

Jack and Jill went up the hill
To fetch a pail of water;
Jack fell down and broke his crown,
And Jill came tumbling after.

Up Jack got, and home did trot,
As fast as he could caper;
He went to bed to mend his head
With vinegar and brown paper.

This rhyme may be based on an old Scandinavian folk tale about two children who were captured by the moon while they were getting water from a well.

GOOSEY, GOOSEY GANDER

Goosey, goosey gander, whither shall I wander?
Upstairs and downstairs and in my lady's chamber.
There I met an old man who would not say his prayers;
I took him by the left leg and threw him down the stairs.

HUMPTY DUMPTY

Humpty Dumpty sat on a wall,
Humpty Dumpty had a great fall;
All the King's horses and all the King's men
Couldn't put Humpty together again.

8

SING A SONG OF SIXPENCE

Sing a song of sixpence, a pocket full of rye;
Four and twenty blackbirds baked in a pie.
When the pie was opened, the birds began to sing,
Wasn't that a dainty dish to set before the King?

The King was in his counting-house, counting out his money;
The Queen was in the parlor, eating bread and honey;
The maid was in the garden, hanging out the clothes,
When down came a blackbird and pecked off her nose.

GIRLS AND BOYS COME OUT TO PLAY

Girls and boys come out to play, The moon doth shine — as bright as day. Leave your sup - per and leave your sleep, And join your play - fel - lows in the street.

Girls and boys come out to play,
The moon doth shine as bright as day.
Leave your supper and leave your sleep,
And join your playfellows in the street.

Come with a whoop, and come with a call,
Come with a good will or not at all.
Up the ladder and down the wall,
A penny loaf will serve us all.

HEY DIDDLE, DIDDLE

Hey diddle, diddle,
The cat and the fiddle,
The cow jumped over the moon;
The little dog laughed
To see such fun,
And the dish ran away with the spoon.

JACK SPRAT

Jack Sprat could eat no fat, His wife could eat no lean, And so be-tween them both, you see, They licked the plat-ter clean.

Jack Sprat could eat no fat,
His wife could eat no lean,
And so between them both, you see,
They licked the platter clean.

LITTLE JACK HORNER

Lit – tle Jack Hor – ner Sat in a cor – ner,

Eat – ing a Christ – mas pie; _____ He put in his thumb, And

pulled out a plum, And said "What a good boy am I".

Little Jack Horner
Sat in a corner,
Eating a Christmas pie;
He put in his thumb,
And pulled out a plum,
And said "What a good boy am I".

ROCK-A-BYE, BABY

Rock-a-bye, baby, on the tree-top,
When the wind blows, the cradle will rock.
When the bough breaks, the cradle will fall,
And down will come baby, cradle and all.

This song is probably about Native Americans. They often put their babies in cradles hung from branches. When the wind blew, it rocked the cradles, sending the babies to sleep.

14

SEE-SAW, MARGERY DAW

See-saw, Margery Daw,
Johnny shall have a new master;
He shall have but a penny a day,
Because he can't work any faster.

Many people think this rhyme was sung by workers sawing wood with a two-handled saw.

15

THERE WAS AN OLD WOMAN WHO LIVED IN A SHOE

There was an old woman who lived in a shoe,
She had so many children she didn't know what to do;
She gave them some broth, without any bread,
Then she whipped them all soundly and put them to bed.

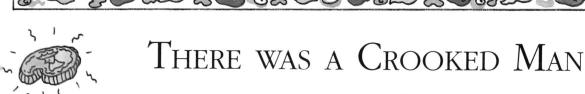

THERE WAS A CROOKED MAN

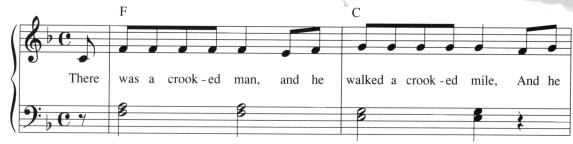

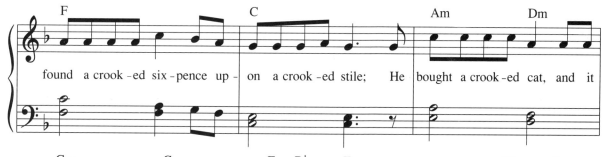

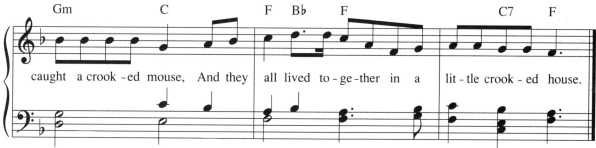

There was a crooked man, and he walked a crooked mile,
And he found a crooked sixpence upon a crooked stile;
He bought a crooked cat, and it caught a crooked mouse,
And they all lived together in a little crooked house.

THE OWL AND THE PUSSY-CAT

The Owl and the Pus-sy-cat went to sea In a beau -ti - ful pea - green boat, They took some hon - ey, and plen -ty of mon -ey, Wrapped up in a five-pound note. The Owl looked up to the stars a - bove, And sang to a small gui-

-tar, "O love - ly Pus - sy, O Pus - sy, my love, _ What a
beau - ti - ful pus - sy you are!"_____ "O love - ly Pus - sy, O
Pus - sy, my love, _ What a beau - ti - ful pus - sy you are!"_____

The Owl and the Pussy-cat went to sea
In a beautiful pea-green boat,
They took some honey, and plenty of money,
Wrapped up in a five-pound note.
The Owl looked up to the stars above,
And sang to a small guitar,
"O lovely Pussy, O Pussy, my love,
What a beautiful pussy you are!"
"O lovely Pussy, O Pussy, my love,
What a beautiful pussy you are!"

RING AROUND THE ROSIES

Ring a - round the ro - sies, A
pock - et full of po - sies. Ash - es!
Ash - es! We all fall down. _____

Ring around the rosies,
A pocket full of posies,
Ashes! Ashes!
We all fall down.

The cows are in the meadow
Lying fast asleep,
Ashes! Ashes!
We all get up again!

RIDE A COCK HORSE

Ride a cock horse to Banbury Cross, To see a fine la-dy up-on a white horse; With rings on her fin-gers and bells on her toes, She shall have mu-sic where-ev-er she goes.

Ride a cock horse to Banbury Cross,
To see a fine lady upon a white horse;
With rings on her fingers and bells on her toes,
She shall have music wherever she goes.

I Had a Little Nut Tree

I had a little nut tree, nothing would it bear,
But a silver nutmeg and a golden pear.
The King of Spain's daughter came to visit me,
And all for the sake of my little nut tree.

THE NORTH WIND DOTH BLOW

The north wind doth blow,
And we shall have snow,
And what will the robin do then, poor thing?
He'll sit in a barn,
And keep himself warm,
And hide his head under his wing, poor thing!

LAVENDER'S BLUE

Lav - en - der's blue, dil - ly, dil - ly, Lav - en - der's green,

When I am King, dil - ly, dil - ly, You shall be Queen.

Lavender's blue, dilly, dilly,
Lavender's green,
When I am King, dilly, dilly,
You shall be Queen.

Call up your men, dilly, dilly,
Set them to work,
Some to the plough, dilly, dilly,
Some to the cart.

Some to make hay, dilly, dilly,
Some to cut corn,
While you and I, dilly, dilly,
Keep ourselves warm.

Lavender's green, dilly, dilly,
Lavender's blue,
If you love me, dilly, dilly,
I will love you.

24

THREE BLIND MICE

Three blind mice, three blind mice,
See how they run! See how they run!
They all ran after the farmer's wife,
Who cut off their tails with a carving knife,
Did ever you see such a thing in your life,
As three blind mice?

TWINKLE, TWINKLE, LITTLE STAR

Twin - kle, twin - kle, lit - tle star, How I won - der what you are, Up a - bove the world so high, Like a dia - mond in the sky. Twin - kle, twin - kle, lit - tle star, How I won - der what you are.

1. Twinkle, twinkle, little star,
How I wonder what you are,
Up above the world so high,
Like a diamond in the sky.
Twinkle, twinkle, little star,
How I wonder what you are.

2. When the blazing sun is gone,
When he nothing shines upon,
Then you show your little light,
Twinkle, twinkle, all the night.
Twinkle, twinkle, little star,
How I wonder what you are.

3. Then the traveller in the dark
Thanks you for your tiny spark.
Could he see which way to go
If you did not twinkle so?
Twinkle, twinkle, little star,
How I wonder what you are.

4. In the dark blue sky you keep,
And often through my curtains peep.
For you never shut your eye
Till the sun is in the sky.
Twinkle, twinkle, little star,
How I wonder what you are.

This song was originally a poem called "The Star". It was written at the beginning of the 19th century.

Pussy-Cat, Pussy-Cat

Pus – sy – cat, pus – sy – cat, where have you been? I've
been up to Lon – don to look at the Queen.
Pus – sy – cat, pus – sy – cat, what did you there? I
fright – ened a lit – tle mouse un – der her chair.

Pussy-cat, pussy-cat, where have you been?
I've been up to London to look at the Queen.
Pussy-cat, pussy-cat, what did you there?
I frightened a little mouse under her chair.

28

Pease Pudding Hot

Pease pud - ding hot,
Pease pud - ding cold,
Pease pud - ding in the pot,
Nine days old.

Pease pudding hot,
Pease pudding cold,
Pease pudding in the pot,
Nine days old.

Some like it hot,
Some like it cold,
Some like it in the pot,
Nine days old.

29

MARY, MARY, QUITE CONTRARY

Ma - ry, Ma - ry, quite con - tra - ry, How does your gar - den grow? With sil - ver bells and cock - le shells, And pret - ty maids all in a row.

Mary, Mary, quite contrary,
How does your garden grow?
With silver bells and cockle shells,
And pretty maids all in a row.

ITSY, BITSY SPIDER

Itsy, bitsy spider climbed up the water spout.
Down came the rain and washed the spider out.
Out came the sunshine, and dried up all the rain,
So itsy, bitsy spider climbed up the spout again.

ONE, TWO, THREE, FOUR, FIVE

One, two, three, four, five,
Once I caught a fish a-live;
Six, sev-en, eight, nine, ten,
Then I let him go a-gain.

For many years this rhyme has been used to help children learn how to count.

One, two, three, four, five,
Once I caught a fish alive;
Six, seven, eight, nine, ten,
Then I let him go again.

Why did you let him go?
Because he bit my finger so.
Which finger did he bite?
This little finger on the right.

HICKORY, DICKORY, DOCK!

Hick - or - y, dick - or - y, dock!
mou - se ran up — the clock. The clock struck one, The
mouse ran down, Hick - or - y, dick - or - y, dock!

Hickory, dickory, dock!
The mouse ran up the clock.
The clock struck one,
The mouse ran down,
Hickory, dickory, dock!

Many people think the words "Hickory, dickory, dock" are part of a counting rhyme used by shepherds to help them count their sheep.

I'm a Little Teapot

I'm a lit – tle tea – pot, short and stout,

Here is my hand – le, here is my spout. When I see the tea – cups,

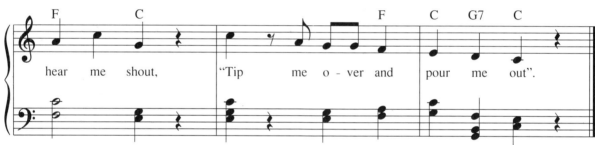

hear me shout, "Tip me o – ver and pour me out".

I'm a little teapot, short and stout,
Here is my handle, here is my spout.
When I see the tea cups, hear me shout,
"Just tip me over and pour me out".

LITTLE TOMMY TUCKER

Little Tommy Tucker,
Sings for his supper
What shall we give him?
White bread and butter.
How shall he cut it
Without e'er a knife?
How will he be married
Without e'er a wife?

Pat-a-Cake, Pat-a-Cake

Pat - a - cake, pat - a - cake, ba - ker's man,

Bake me a cake just as fast as you can. Pat it and prick it, and

mark it with B, And put it in the ov - en for ba - by and me.

Pat-a-cake, pat-a-cake, baker's man,
Bake me a cake just as fast as you can.
Pat it and prick it, and mark it with B,
And put it in the oven for baby and me.

Baa, Baa, Black Sheep

Baa, baa, black sheep, Have you an-y wool? Yes, sir, yes, sir,

Three bags full; One for the mas-ter, And one for the dame, And

one for the lit-tle boy Who lives down the lane.

Baa, baa, black sheep,
Have you any wool?
Yes, sir, yes, sir,
Three bags full;
One for the master,
And one for the dame,
And one for the little boy
Who lives down the lane.

MARY HAD A LITTLE LAMB

Mary had a little lamb,
Little lamb, little lamb,
Mary had a little lamb,
It's fleece was white as snow;

*The words to this rhyme
were written in about
1830. At that time,
farmers' children often
adopted lambs as pets, so
the story may be true.*

And everywhere that Mary went,
Mary went, Mary went,
Everywhere that Mary went,
The lamb was sure to go.

It followed her to school one day,
School one day, school one day,
It followed her to school one day,
That was against the rule;

It made the children laugh and play,
Laugh and play, laugh and play,
It made the children laugh and play,
To see a lamb at school.

And so the teacher turned it out,
Turned it out, turned it out,
So the teacher turned it out,
But still it lingered near;

And waited for her patiently,
Patiently, patiently,
Waited for her patiently,
Till Mary did appear.

"Why does the lamb love Mary so?
Mary so? Mary so?
Why does the lamb love Mary so?"
The eager children cry;

"Why, Mary loves the lamb, you know,
Lamb, you know, lamb, you know,
Mary loves the lamb, you know",
The teacher did reply.

CURLY LOCKS

Cur - ly Locks, Cur - ly Locks, Wilt thou be mine? Thou

shalt not wash dish - es Nor yet feed the swine, But sit on a cush - ion And

sew a fine seam, And feed up - on straw - ber - ries, Su - gar and cream.

Curly Locks, Curly Locks,
Wilt thou be mine?
Thou shalt not wash dishes
Nor yet feed the swine,
But sit on a cushion
And sew a fine seam,
And feed upon strawberries,
Sugar and cream.

LUCY LOCKET

Lucy Locket lost her pocket,
Kitty Fisher found it;
But not a penny was there in it,
Only ribbon round it.

COCK-A-DOODLE-DOO!

Cock - a - doo - dle - doo! _____ My
dame has lost her shoe, _____ My mas - ter's lost his
fidd - ling stick, And does - n't know what to do.

Cock-a-doodle-doo!
My dame has lost her shoe,
My master's lost his fiddling stick,
And doesn't know what to do.

Cock-a-doodle-doo!
My dame has found her shoe,
My master's found his fiddling stick,
So cock-a-doodle-doo!

LITTLE MISS MUFFET

Lit - tle Miss Muf - fet Sat on a tuf - fet,

Eat - ing her curds and whey; ____ A - long came a spi - der, Who

sat down be - side her, And frigh - tened Miss Muf - fet a - way.

Little Miss Muffet
Sat on a tuffet,
Eating her curds and whey;
Along came a spider,
Who sat down beside her,
And frightened Miss Muffet away.

LITTLE BO-PEEP

Lit – tle Bo – peep has lost her sheep, And does – n't know where _ to find them; Leave them a – lone, and they'll come home, Wag – ging their tails _ be – hind them.

44

Little Bo-peep has lost her sheep,
And doesn't know where to find them;
Leave them alone, and they'll come home,
Wagging their tails behind them.

Little Bo-peep fell fast asleep,
And dreamed she heard them bleating;
But when she awoke, she found it a joke,
For they were still a-fleeting.

Then up she took her little crook,
Determined for to find them;
She found them indeed, but it made her heart bleed,
For they'd left their tails behind them.

It happened one day, as Bo-peep did stray
Into a meadow hard by;
There she espied their tails side by side,
All hung on a tree to dry.

She heaved a sigh, and wiped her eye,
And over the hillocks went rambling;
And tried what she could, as a shepherdess should,
To tack again each to its lambkin.

Bo-peep is an old name for the game of hide and seek.

Hot Cross Buns!

Hot cross buns!

Hot cross buns!

One a pen-ny, two a pen-ny, Hot cross buns!

If you have no daugh-ters,

Give them to your sons;

One a pen-ny, two a pen-ny, Hot cross buns!

This rhyme was often sung by bakers at their market stalls.

Hot cross buns!
Hot cross buns!
One a penny, two a penny,
Hot cross buns!
If you have no daughters,
Give them to your sons;
One a penny, two a penny,
Hot cross buns!

Hot cross buns are sweet, spiced bread rolls with a cross marked on top. They are traditionally eaten on Good Friday (the Friday before Easter).

SIMPLE SIMON

Sim - ple Si - mon met a pie - man Go - ing to the fair; ___ Said
Sim - ple Si - mon to the pie - man, "Let me taste your ware".

Simple Simon met a pieman
Going to the fair;
Said Simple Simon to the pieman,
"Let me taste your ware".

Said the pieman unto Simon,
"Show me first your penny";
Said Simple Simon to the pieman,
"Sir, I haven't any".

Simple Simon went a-fishing
For to catch a whale;
But all the water that he had
Was in his mother's pail.

Simple Simon went to look
If plums grew on a thistle;
He pricked his fingers very much,
Which made poor Simon whistle.

Games

Some of the nursery rhymes in this book have actions or games that go with them. You can find out about these below.

Hickory, Dickory, Dock

You can use this rhyme to decide who starts a game. As you say the words, point at each player in turn. When the rhyme ends, the person you are pointing at starts the game.

Pat-a-Cake, Pat-a-Cake

Clap your hands while you sing the first line, and rub them together in the second line. Next, pretend to prick one of your hands with the first finger of the other. Then, as you sing the last line, pretend you are putting a cake into the oven.

Humpty Dumpty

Sit down on the floor with your knees against your chest and wrap your arms around your knees. Begin singing, and rock gently backward and forward. When you reach the line "Humpty Dumpty had a great fall", roll over backward. Keep singing, and without letting go of your knees, try to sit upright again. (This is harder than it sounds!) The player who does this first is the winner.

Pease Pudding Hot

This rhyme can be used as a clapping game. To play, you have to stand facing a partner. There are four different clapping movements.

1. Clap your own hands together.
2. Clap your right hand against your partner's right hand.
3. Clap your left hand against your partner's left hand.
4. Clap both hands against your partner's hands. Repeat this, singing faster little by little, until one of you makes a mistake.

I'm a Little Teapot

When you sing "Here is my handle", put one hand on your hip. When you sing "here is my spout", put your other arm out like the spout of a teapot. During the last line, lean sideways as if you are pouring the tea.

Ring Around the Rosies

While you sing this rhyme, all hold hands and move around in a circle. When you sing "We all fall down", crouch down as low as you can. Then, as you sing "We all get up again!", jump up as high as you can.

Guitar Chords

The diagrams below show you how to play all the guitar chords used in this book. The vertical lines represent the strings (the lowest on the left) and the horizontal lines are the frets (the top thick line is the nut). The black circles show you where to press the strings, and the numbers beneath tell you which left-hand fingers to use. An o above a string tells you to play it without using any left-hand fingers and an x means you don't play the string at all. A curved line tells you to press a finger across more than one string.

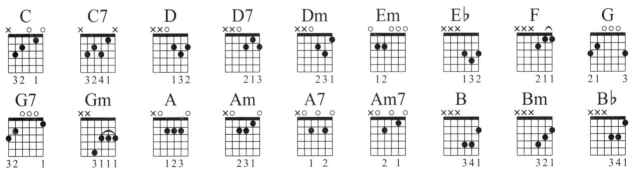

First published in 1996 by Usborne Publishing Ltd, Usborne House, 83-85 Saffron Hill, London, EC1N 8RT, England.
Printed in Spain. AE First published in America March 1997.